MORE

Brit Wit

The perfect riposte for every social occasion

summersdale

MORE BRIT WIT

Summersdale Publishers Ltd
46 West Street
Chichester
West Sussex
PO19 1RP
UK

www.summersdale.com

Disclaimer
Every effort has been made to obtain the necessary permissions with reference to copyright material, both illustrative and quoted; should there be any omissions in this respect we apologise and shall be pleased to make the appropriate acknowledgements in any future edition.

Printed and bound in Great Britain

ISBN 1 84024 464 X

Editor's Note

The best of British wit: there's nothing quite like it, whether you're a lover of language or simply want to impress. A date, a dinner, a wedding, an argument, a presentation, an essay – there are occasions galore when an amusing quip is worth its weight in gold.

Thanks to popular demand, we're delighted to present this second compendium of the funniest quotations from across the centuries right up to today. We've found even more of the sharpest barbs on topics ranging from art to drinking to Brits themselves. When it comes to families, marriage and religion, sometimes you've just got to laugh.

Oddly enough, British Prime Ministers seem to produce some of the wittiest (and cattiest) remarks, while the differences between the sexes always yield a fresh crop of deliciously obnoxious observations. And naturally, there's a special place for insults and rude ripostes to impress your friends and crush your enemies.

They all add up to a superb array of Brit wit, and we trust you'll derive hours of pleasure from browsing through this book. After all, as Thomas Love Peacock said in the nineteenth century, 'A book that furnishes no quotations is no book – it is a plaything.'

Contents

MORE
Brit Wit

Hot water is my
native element.
I was in it as a baby,
and I have never
seemed to get out
of it ever since.

Edith Sitwell, poet (1887–1964)

Advice

Have the courage to be ignorant
of a great number of things, in
order to avoid the calamity of
being ignorant of everything.
Sydney Smith, essayist (1771–1845)

The only way to be sure of catching
a train is to miss the one before it.
G. K. Chesterton, writer (1874–1936)

There is no such whetstone, to
sharpen a good wit and encourage
a will to learning, as is praise.
Roger Ascham, writer (1515–1568)

Don't give a woman advice: one should never give a woman anything she can't wear in the evening.

Oscar Wilde, poet, novelist, dramatist and critic
(1854–1900), *An Ideal Husband*, 1895

If a thing's worth doing,
it's worth doing badly.

G. K. Chesterton

Good but rarely came
from good advice.

Lord Byron, Romantic poet and satirist (1788–1824)

Moderation is a fatal thing
– nothing succeeds like excess.

Oscar Wilde, *A Woman of No Importance*, 1893

———•———

When a man wants your advice,
he generally wants your praise.

Lord Chesterfield, statesman,
diplomat and wit (1694–1773)

———•———

The worst men often
give the best advice.

Francis Bacon, lawyer and philosopher (1561–1626)

———•———

Never try to reason the
prejudice out of a man. It was
not reasoned into him, and
cannot be reasoned out.

Sydney Smith

Action may
not always bring
happiness; but there
is no happiness
without action.

Benjamin Disraeli, former Prime Minister
and novelist (1804–1881)

Age

You only have to survive in England and all is forgiven... if you can eat a boiled egg at 90 in England they think you deserve a Nobel Prize.

Alan Bennett, playwright, writer and actor

Mrs Allonby: I delight in men over seventy, they always offer one the devotion of a lifetime.

Oscar Wilde, *A Woman of No Importance*

One should never trust a woman who tells one her real age. A woman who would tell one that would tell one anything.

Oscar Wilde, *A Woman of No Importance*

I do wish I could tell you my age but it's impossible. It keeps changing all the time.

Greer Garson, actress (1908–1996)

Life begins at 40 – but so do fallen arches, rheumatism, faulty eyesight, and the tendency to tell a story to the same person, three or four times.

Helen Rowland, English-American writer (1876–1950)

He was either a man of 150 who was rather young for his years, or a man of 110 who had been aged by trouble.

P. G. Wodehouse, humorist and writer (1881–1975), *Lord Emsworth Acts for the Best*, 1937

Youth is a blunder; manhood
a struggle; old age a regret.

Benjamin Disraeli

———•———

I wanna live 'til I die, no more, no less.

Eddie Izzard, stand-up comedian and actor

What I am looking for is a blessing not in disguise.

Jerome K. Jerome, humour writer (1859–1927)

Animals

The great pleasure of a dog
is that you may make a fool of
yourself with him and not only
will he not scold you, but he will
make a fool of himself too.

Samuel Butler, author (1835–1902)

———•———

Dogs look up to us. Cats look
down on us. Pigs treat us as equals.

Winston Churchill, statesman, author and Prime
Minister during World War II (1874–1965)

When my cats aren't happy, I'm
not happy. Not because I care
about their mood but because
I know they're just sitting there
thinking up ways to get even.

Percy Bysshe Shelley, Romantic poet (1792–1822)

Men! The only animal
in the world to fear.

D. H. Lawrence, poet, novelist
and essayist (1885–1930)

Man is an animal that makes
bargains: no other animal
does this – no dog exchanges
bones with another.

Adam Smith, philosopher and economist (1723–1790)

If you eliminate smoking and gambling, you will be amazed to find that almost all an Englishman's pleasures can be, and mostly are, shared by his dog.

George Bernard Shaw, playwright and essayist (1856–1950)

Cats have nine lives. Which makes them ideal for experimentation.

Jimmy Carr, comedian and television presenter

A horse is dangerous at both ends and uncomfortable in the middle.

Ian Fleming, author (1908–1964)

It is a conspiracy of silence against me – a conspiracy of silence. What should I do?

Join it.

Exchange between Lewis Morris, poet
(1833–1907) and Oscar Wilde

Arts

I do not have much patience with a thing of beauty that must be explained to be understood. If it does need additional interpretation by someone other than the creator, then I question whether it has fulfilled its purpose.

Charlie Chaplin, comic artist (1889–1977)

Acting is merely the art of keeping a large group of people from coughing.

Ralph Richardson, actor (1902–1983)

The moral of filmmaking in Britain is that you will be screwed by the weather.

Hugh Grant, actor

Nothing is capable of being well
set to music that is not nonsense

Joseph Addison, politician (1672–1719)

———◆———

Spielberg isn't a filmmaker,
he's a confectioner.

Alex Cox, film director and actor

———◆———

Acting is not very hard. The
most important things are to
be able to laugh and cry.

Glenda Jackson, actress and politician

I've half a mind to tumble
down to prose,
But verse is more in
fashion - so here goes.

Lord Byron, poet (1788-1824)

Kant and Hegel are interesting
thinkers. But I am happy to insist
that they are also terrible writers.

Alain de Botton, writer

A great many people now reading
and writing would be better
employed keeping rabbits.

Edith Sitwell

The reason why so few good books
are written is that so few people
who can write know anything.

Walter Bagehot, political analyst,
economist and editor (1826–1877)

It is all very well to be able
to write books, but can
you waggle your ears?

J. M. Barrie, playwright and author
(1860–1937) to H.G. Wells

Everything's got a moral,
if only you can find it.

Lewis Carroll, writer (1832–1898), *Alice's
Adventures in Wonderland*, 1865

Some who have read the book,
or at any rate have reviewed it,
have found it boring, absurd,
or contemptible; and I have
no cause to complain, since I
have similar opinions of their
works, or of the kinds of writing
that they evidently prefer.

J. R. R. Tolkien, author (1892–1973)

Writing is like getting married.
One should never commit oneself
until one is amazed at one's luck.

Iris Murdoch, novelist and philosopher
(1919–1999) *The Black Prince*, 1973

Good prose is like a windowpane

George Orwell, novelist and essayist (1903–1950)

I know not, sir, whether Bacon wrote the works of Shakespeare, but if he did not it seems to me that he missed the opportunity of his life.

J. M. Barrie

If you write fiction you are, in a sense, corrupted. There's a tremendous corruptibility for the fiction writer because you're dealing mainly with sex and violence. These remain the basic themes, they're the basic themes of Shakespeare whether you like it or not.

Anthony Burgess, novelist and critic (1917–1993)

Writing is easy. You only need to stare at a piece of blank paper until your forehead bleeds

Douglas Adams, comic writer (1952–2001)

I take the view, and always have, that if you cannot say what you are going to say in 20 minutes you ought go to away and write a book about it

Lord Brabazon, aviator (1884–1964)

There is a great discovery still
to be made in literature, that
of paying literary men by the
quantity they do not write

Thomas Carlyle, historian and essayist (1795–1881)

———

Unprovided with original learning,
unformed in the habits of thinking,
unskilled in the arts of composition,
I resolved to write a book.

Edward Gibbon, historian (1737–1794)

———

Write how you want, the
critic shall show the world you
could have written better.

Oliver Goldsmith, Irish-born essayist, poet,
novelist and dramatist (1730–1774)

Literature is mostly about having
sex and not much about having
children; life is the other way round.

David Lodge, critic and novelist

I hate vulgar realism in literature.
The man who could call a spade a
spade should be compelled to use
one. It is the only thing he is fit for.

Oscar Wilde, *The Picture of Dorian Gray*, 1891

No human being ever spoke of
scenery for above two minutes at a
time, which makes me suspect that
we hear too much of it in literature.

Robert Louis Stevenson, author (1850–1894)

Reviewers are usually people who would have been, poets, historians, biographer, if they could. They have tried their talents at one thing or another and have failed; therefore they turn critic.

Samuel Taylor Coleridge

———•———

A historical romance is the only kind of book where chastity really counts.

Barbara Cartland, author (1901–2000)

———•———

For most of history, Anonymous was a woman.

Virginia Woolf, writer (1882–1941)

Writing about music is like dancing
about architecture – it's a really
stupid thing to want to do.

Elvis Costello, songwriter, musician and singer

You just pick up a chord, go
twang, and you've got music.

Sid Vicious, bassist for the Sex Pistols (1957–1979)

To generalise is
to be an idiot.

William Blake, poet, painter and
visionary mystic (1757–1827)

Beauty

Beauty is all very well at first sight;
but who ever looks at it when it has
been in the house three days?

George Bernard Shaw

———•———

A witty woman is a treasure;
a witty beauty is a power.

George Meredith, poet and novelist (1828–1909)

———•———

Beauty is an outward gift which is
seldom despised, except by those
to whom it has been refused.

Edward Gibbon

To look almost pretty is an
acquisition of higher delight
to a girl who has been looking
plain for the first fifteen years
of her life than a beauty from
her cradle can ever receive.

Jane Austen, novelist (1775–1817),
Northanger Abbey, 1817

Nonsense and beauty have
close connections.

E. M. Forster, novelist and essayist (1879–1970)

Beauty ought to look a little
surprised: it is the emotion that
best suits her face. The beauty
who does not look surprised,
who accepts her position as
her due – she reminds us too
much of a prima donna.

E. M. Forster

It is hard, if not impossible, to snub
a beautiful woman – they remain
beautiful and the snub recoils.

Winston Churchill

———•———

A poor beauty finds more
lovers than husbands.

**George Herbert, metaphysical poet
and clergyman (1593–1633)**

———•———

Familiarity is a magician that is cruel
to beauty but kind to ugliness.

**Ouida, aka Marie Louise De La
Ramee, novelist (1839–1908)**

———•———

The saying that beauty is but skin
deep is but a skin deep saying.

**John Ruskin, writer and critic of art
and architecture (1819–1900)**

The problem with
beauty is that it's
like being born rich
and getting poorer.

Joan Collins, actress

Beauty is Nature's coin, must not be hoarded, But must be current.

John Milton, poet and scholar (1608–1674)

It is well known that Beauty does not look with a good grace on the timid advances of Humour.

W. Somerset Maugham, short-story writer, novelist and playwright (1874–1965)

A bachelor never quite gets over the idea that he is a thing of beauty and a boy forever.

Helen Rowland

It is only shallow people who do
not judge by appearances.

Oscar Wilde, *The Picture of Dorian Gray*

———

Miss Brooke had that kind of
beauty which seems to be thrown
into relief by poor dress.

George Eliot, novelist (1819–1880), *Middlemarch*

———

If a woman rebels against high-
heeled shoes, she should take
care to do it in a very smart hat.

George Bernard Shaw

She wore far too much rouge
last night and not quite enough
clothes. That is always a sign
of despair in a woman.

Oscar Wilde, *An Ideal Husband*

It is dangerous for mortal beauty,
or terrestrial virtue, to be examined
by too strong a light. The torch of
Truth shows much that we cannot,
and all that we would not, see.

Samuel Johnson, poet, critic and writer (1709–1784)

The one great
principle of the
English law is to make
business for itself.

Charles Dickens, novelist (1812–1870), *Bleak House*

Britain and the British

An Irishman fights before he reasons, a Scotchman reasons before he fights, an Englishman is not particular as to the order of precedence, but will do either to accommodate his customers.

Charles Caleb Colton, sportsman
and writer (1780–1832)

As a rule they will refuse even to sample a foreign dish, they regard such things as garlic and olive oil with disgust, life is unliveable to them unless they have tea and puddings.

George Orwell

The English contribution to world cuisine – the chip.

John Cleese, comic actor

Oats. A grain, which in England is generally given to horses, but in Scotland supports the people.

Samuel Johnson

The whole strength of England lies in the fact that the enormous majority of the English people are snobs.

George Bernard Shaw

What Englishman will give his mind to politics as long as he can afford to keep a motor car?

George Bernard Shaw

England is unrivalled for two
things – sport and politics.

Benjamin Disraeli

———•———

I think the British have the
distinction above all other nations
of being able to put new wine into
old bottles without bursting them.

**Clement Attlee, statesman and former
Prime Minister (1883–1967)**

———•———

Thinking is the most unhealthy
thing in the world, and people
die of it just as they die of any
other disease. Fortunately, in
England at any rate, thought
is not catching. Our splendid
physique as a people is entirely
due to our national stupidity.

Oscar Wilde, *The Decay of Lying*, 1889

It is illegal in England to
state in print that a wife can
and should derive sexual
pleasure from intercourse.

Bertrand Russell, logician, philosopher and social
critic (1872–1970), *Marriage and Morals*, 1932

———————

Propose to any Englishman any
principle or instrument, however
admirable, and you will observe that
the whole effort of the English
mind is directed to find a difficulty,
a defect, or an impossibility in it.

Charles Babbage, mathematician
and inventor (1791–1871)

The difference between the vanity of a Frenchman and an Englishman seems to be this: The one thinks everything right that is French, the other thinks everything wrong that is not English.

William Hazlitt, essayist (1778–1830)

———•———

Scotland: A land of meanness, sophistry and lust.

Lord Byron

———•———

It took me 20 years of studied self-restraint, aided by the natural decay of my faculties, to make myself dull enough to be accepted as a serious person by the British public.

George Bernard Shaw

The Irish are hearty, the Scotch plausible, the French polite, the Germans good-natured, the Italians courtly, the Spaniards reserved and decorous – the English alone seem to exist in taking and giving offense.

William Hazlitt

The English people on the whole are surely the nicest people in the world, and everybody makes everything so easy for everyone else, that there is almost nothing to resist at all.

D. H. Lawrence

A truth that's told
with bad intent
Beats all the lies
you can invent.

William Blake

Death

When I look back on all these worries, I remember the story of the old man who said on his deathbed that he had had a lot of trouble in his life, most of which had never happened.

Winston Churchill

Nothing in his life became him like the leaving it.

William Shakespeare, playwright and poet (1564–1616), *Macbeth*

I have wrestled with death. It is the most unexciting contest you can imagine

Joseph Conrad, writer (1857–1924)

Either that wallpaper goes, or I do.

Attributed to Oscar Wilde, as he lay dying in Paris

———•———

I told you I was ill.

Spike Milligan, comic writer and
performer (1918–2002)

———•———

The man that runs away
Lives to die another day.

A. E. Housman, poet and scholar
(1859–1936) *A Shropshire Lad*, 1896

There will always be death
and taxes; however, death
doesn't get worse every year.

Unknown

He'd make a lovely corpse.

Charles Dickens, *David Copperfield*

Most people would rather die
than think; in fact, they do so.

Bertrand Russell

Courage is almost a contradiction in terms. It means a strong desire to live taking the form of readiness to die.

G. K. Chesterton

He is one of those people who would be enormously improved by death.

Saki, aka Hector Hugo Munro, short-story writer (1870–1916)

All progress is based
upon a universal
innate desire of
every organism to live
beyond its income.

Samuel Butler

Drinking

I can resist everything
except temptation.

Oscar Wilde, *Lady Windermere's Fan*, 1892

Work is the curse of the
drinking classes.

Attributed to Oscar Wilde

And wine can of their
wits the wise beguile,
Make the sage frolic, and
the serious smile.

Alexander Pope, poet and satirist (1688–1744)

Pure water is the best of gifts
that man to man can bring.
But who am I that I should
have the best of anything?
Let princes revel at the pump,
let peers with ponds make free,
Whisky, or wine, or even beer
is good enough for me.

Lord Neaves, Rector of St. Andrews
University (1800–1876)

A good local pub has much in
common with a church, except
that a pub is warmer, and
there's more conversation.

William Blake

Alcohol is a very necessary article.
It enables Parliament to do things at
eleven at night that no sane person
would do at eleven in the morning.

George Bernard Shaw

———•———

The first draught serveth for health,
the second for pleasure, the third
for shame, the fourth for madness.

Walter Raleigh, explorer (1552–1618)

———•———

The road of excess leads
to the palace of wisdom.

William Blake

This is one of the disadvantages
of wine; it makes a man mistake
words for thoughts.

Samuel Johnson

I'm not a heavy drinker; I
can sometimes go for hours
without touching a drop.

**Noël Coward, actor, dramatist and
songwriter (1899–1973)**

An alcoholic is anyone you don't
like who drinks as much as you do.

Dylan Thomas, poet (1914–1953)

Drink is the feast of reason
and the flow of soul.

Alexander Pope

———◆———

The best beer is where priests
go to drink. For a quart of
Ale is a dish for a King.

William Shakespeare, *A Winter's Tale*

———◆———

As he brews so shall he drink.

Ben Jonson, playwright (1572–1637)

Light beer is an
invention of the
Prince of Darkness.

John Thaw, actor (1942–2002) *Inspector Morse*

Education

Education is simply the soul
of a society as it passes from
one generation to another.

G. K. Chesterton

Education is what remains
when we have forgotten all
that we have been taught.

George Savile, statesman and author (1633–1695)

Education makes a people easy to
lead, but difficult to drive; easy to
govern but impossible to enslave.

Henry Peter Brougham, politician, reformer
and former Lord Chancellor (1778–1868)

The more scholastically educated
a man is generally, the more
he is an emotional boor.

D. H. Lawrence

If one could only teach the
English how to talk, and the
Irish how to listen, society here
would be quite civilised.

Oscar Wilde, *An Ideal Husband*

The great mass of humanity should
never learn to read or write.

D. H. Lawrence

When we are planning for posterity, we ought to remember that virtue is not hereditary.

Thomas Paine, intellectual, scholar and idealist (1737–1809)

The sum and substance of female education in America, as in England, is training women to consider marriage as the sole object in life, and to pretend that they do not think so.

Harriet Martineau, writer and social reformer (1802–1876)

He's very clever, but sometimes
his brains go to his head.

**Margot Asquith, writer and wife of former Prime
Minister Herbert Asquith (1864–1945)**

———•———

Experience is the hardest kind
of teacher. It gives you the test
first, and the lesson afterward.

Anonymous

George Bernard Shaw to Winston Churchill: Am reserving two tickets for you for my premiere. Come and bring a friend – if you have one.

Churchill: Impossible to be present for the first performance. Will attend second – if there is one.

Families and Friends

Whether family life is physically
harmful is still in dispute.

Keith Waterhouse, novelist, columnist and playwright,
The Passing of the Third-floor Buck, 1974

I can't help detesting my relations. I
suppose it comes from the fact that
none of us can stand other people
having the same faults as ourselves.

Oscar Wilde, *The Picture of Dorian Gray*

Relations are just a tedious
pack of people, who haven't
got the remotest knowledge
of how to live, nor the smallest
instinct about when to die.

Oscar Wilde, *The Importance of Being Earnest*, 1895

Family jokes, though rightly
cursed by strangers, are the bond
that keeps most families alive.

Stella Benson, writer (1892–1933)

He's my friend that speaks
well of me behind my back.

Thomas Fuller, clergyman and writer (1608–1661)

You find out who your real
friends are when you're
involved in a scandal.

Elizabeth Taylor, actress

———————

Thy friendship oft has made
my heart to ache; do be my
enemy, for friendship's sake.

William Blake

An acquaintance that begins
with a compliment is sure to
develop into a real friendship.
Attributed to Oscar Wilde

Important families are like potatoes.
The best parts are underground.
Francis Bacon

Letter writing is
the only device for
combining solitude
with good company.

Lord Byron

Fashion

I'm not that interested in fashion...
When someone says that lime-green
is the new black for this season, you
just want to tell them to get a life.

Bruce Oldfield, fashion designer

———◆———

What a deformed thief
this fashion is.

William Shakespeare, *Much Ado About Nothing*

———◆———

Fashion is what you adopt when
you don't know who you are.

Quentin Crisp, author (1908–1999)

In words, as fashions, the
same rule will hold,
Alike fantastic if too new or old:
Be not the first by whom
the new are tried,
Nor yet the last to lay the old aside.

Alexander Pope

As to matters of dress, I would
recommend one never to be first in
the fashion nor the last out of it.

John Wesley, evangelist (1703–1791)

It is only the modern that ever
becomes old fashioned.

Oscar Wilde, *The Decay of Lying*

Ladies of Fashion starve their
happiness to feed their vanity,
and their love to feed their pride.

Charles Caleb Colton

———•———

Report of fashions in proud Italy
Whose manners still our
tardy-apish nation
Limps after in base imitation.

William Shakespeare, *The Life and
Death of King Richard The Second*

Fashion is gentility running
away from vulgarity and
afraid of being overtaken.

William Hazlitt

Fashion is the science of
appearance, and it inspires one with
the desire to seem rather than to be.

Henry Fielding, playwright and novelist (1707–1754)

One had as good be out of the
world, as out of the fashion.

Colley Cibber, actor and playwright (1671–1757)

Mediocrity can
talk, but it is for
genius to observe.

Benjamin Disraeli

Foreigners

People travel for the same
reason they collect works of art:
because the best people do it.

Aldous Huxley, novelist and critic (1894–1963)

Travel, in the younger sort,
is a part of education; in the
elder, a part of experience.

Francis Bacon

Americans adore me and will
go on adoring me until I say
something nice about them

George Bernard Shaw

The proper means of increasing the love we bear our native country is to reside some time in a foreign one

William Shenstone, poet and landscape gardener (1714–1763)

I don't hold with abroad and think that foreigners speak English when our backs are turned.

Quentin Crisp

In Russia a man is called a reactionary if he objects to having his property stolen and his wife and children murdered.

Winston Churchill

You can always count on
Americans to do the right thing
– after they've tried everything else.

Winston Churchill

———•———

I love Americans, but not
when they try to talk French.
What a blessing it is that they
never try to talk English.

Saki

———•———

San Francisco is a mad city
– inhabited for the most part by
perfectly insane people whose
women are of remarkable beauty.

**Rudyard Kipling, short-story writer,
poet, and novelist (1865–1936)**

India is a geographical term.
It is no more a united nation
than the Equator.

Winston Churchill

The USA is so enormous,
and so numerous are its schools,
colleges and religious seminaries,
many devoted to special religious
beliefs ranging from the unorthodox
to the dotty, that we can hardly
wonder at its yielding a more
bounteous harvest of gobb.

Peter B. Medawar, zoologist (1915–1987)

One of the minor peculiarities of an Indian tour is the sheer hopelessness that attends any search for a drinkable cup of tea, although this is the land that contains Darjeeling and Ceylon. Neither prayers nor threats will make the Indian servant on the railways or in hotels believe that every Englishman does not like his tea *ystrang* – that is to say, of such a consistency that I could easily have written this book by filling my fountain pen from the teapot... It is strange that the British, who in their time succeeded in imposing so many of their institutions on their Imperial possessions, should have failed over this. It is as if the Indians said: "You have conquered us in other ways; in this one thing, a thing moreover very close to your hearts, we defy you!"

Marco Pallis, traveller and writer (1895–1990) *Peaks and Lamas*, 1938

England is a paradise
for women and hell
for horses; Italy is a
paradise for horses,
hell for women, as
the diverb goes.

Robert Burton, writer and clergyman (1577–1640)

Little things affect little minds.

Benjamin Disraeli

Insults

She had much in common with
Hitler, only no moustache.

Noël Coward

This man I thought had been
a Lord among wits; but, I find,
he is only a wit among Lords.

Samuel Johnson of Lord Chesterfield

Nature, not content with denying
him the ability to think, has endowed
him with the ability to write.

A. E. Housman

He's a sheep in sheep's clothing...
A modest little person, with
much to be modest about.

Winston Churchill

Harold Wilson is going around
the country stirring up apathy.

William Whitelaw, politician (1918–1999)

I regard you with an indifference
bordering on aversion.

Robert Louis Stevenson

He had occasional flashes of
silence, that made his conversation
perfectly delightful.
Sydney Smith

A brain of feathers, and
a heart of lead.
Alexander Pope

I thought men like that
shot themselves.
King George V (1865–1936)

At every crisis the Kaiser crumpled.
In defeat he fled; in revolution he
abdicated; in exile he remarried.

Winston Churchill

He's completely
unspoiled by failure.

Noël Coward

I see her as one great stampede of
lips directed at the nearest derrière.

Noël Coward

She was a large woman
who seemed not so much
dressed as upholstered.

J. M. Barrie

———•———

She spends her day powdering her
face till she looks like a bled pig.

Margot Asquith

———•———

Fine words! I wonder
where you stole them.

Jonathan Swift, poet and satirist (1667–1745)

How low am I, thou painted
maypole? speak;
How low am I? I am not yet so low
But that my nails can
reach unto thine eyes.

William Shakespeare, *A Midsummer Night's Dream*

———•———

Why don't you write books
people can read?

**Nora Joyce (1884–1951) to her husband
James Joyce, author (1882–1941)**

———•———

He is brilliant to the
top of his boots.

**David Lloyd George, Liberal MP and
former Prime Minister (1863–1945)**

He never said a foolish
thing nor did a wise one.

John Wilmot, Second Earl of
Rochester, poet (1647–1680)

———•••———

The right honourable gentleman is
reminiscent of a poker. The only
difference is that a poker gives off
the occasional signs of warmth.

Benjamin Disraeli on Robert Peel

The tautness
of his face sours
ripe grapes.
William Shakespeare

Get you gone, you dwarf;
You minimus, of hindering
knot-grass made;
You bead, you acorn.

William Shakespeare, *A Midsummer Night's Dream*

———◆———

This woman did not fly to
extremes; she lived there.

Quentin Crisp

———◆———

Some folks are wise and
some are otherwise.

Tobias George Smollett, writer (1721–1771)

She plunged into a sea of
platitudes, and with the powerful
breaststroke of a channel swimmer,
made her confident way towards
the white cliffs of the obvious.

W. Somerset Maugham

Only dull people are
brilliant at breakfast.

Oscar Wilde, *An Ideal Husband*

She tells enough white lies
to ice a wedding cake.

Margot Asquith

Better than cystitis.

Jo Brand, comedian, talking about slogans that could
boost British Prime Minister John Major's popularity.

If I say that he is extremely
stupid. I don't mean that in a
derogatory sense. I simply mean
that he's not very intelligent.

Alan Bennett

It's like being savaged
by a dead sheep.

**Dennis Healey, ex-Labour MP on Geoffrey
Howe, former Conservative MP**

He brings to the fierce
struggle of politics the tepid
enthusiasm of a lazy summer
afternoon at a cricket match.

Aneurin Bevan, politician (1897–1960)

He is influenced by infection,
catching an opinion like a cold.

John Ruskin

He was born stupid, and greatly
increased his birthright.

Samuel Butler

He was distinguished for
ignorance; for he had only one
idea and that was wrong.

Benjamin Disraeli

His voice was the most obnoxious
squeak I ever was tormented with.

Charles Lamb, author and critic (1775–1834)

Is he just doing a bad Elvis
pout, or was he born that way?

Freddie Mercury, musician (1946–1991) on Billy Idol

The stupid person's idea
of a clever person.

Elizabeth Bowen, Anglo-Irish writer
(1899–1973) on Aldous Huxley

The human race
has been set
up. Someone,
somewhere, is playing
a practical joke on us.
Apparently, women
need to feel loved to
have sex. Men need
to have sex to feel
loved. How do we
ever get started?

Billy Connolly, actor and comedian

Life

You only require two things in
life: your sanity and your wife.

Tony Blair, Prime Minister

All animals, except man, know
that the principal business
of life is to enjoy it.

Samuel Butler

Any 20 year-old who isn't a
liberal doesn't have a heart,
and any 40 year-old who isn't a
conservative doesn't have a brain.

Winston Churchill

———◆———

Life is like playing a violin
solo in public and learning the
instrument as one goes on.

Samuel Butler

———◆———

Life is wasted on the living.

Douglas Adams

And so, from hour to
hour, we ripe and ripe,
And then from hour to
hour, we rot and rot.

William Shakespeare, *As You Like It*

The trouble with the world is
that the stupid are cocksure and
the intelligent full of doubt.

Bertrand Russell

It is in life as it is in ways, the
shortest way is commonly the
foulest, and surely the fairer
way is not much about.

Francis Bacon

Life is the art of drawing
sufficient conclusions from
insufficient premises.
Samuel Butler

We make a living by what we get,
but we make a life by what we give.
Winston Churchill

Life is one
long process of
getting tired.

Samuel Butler

When we are born, we
cry that we are come
To this great stage of fools.

William Shakespeare, *As You Like It*

Life is not an exact
science, it is an art.

Samuel Butler

Man alone is born crying, lives
complaining, and dies disappointed.

Samuel Johnson

———

My school days were the happiest
days of my life; which should give
you some indication of the misery
I've endured over the past 25 years.

Paul Merton, comedy actor and screen writer

———

The life of every man is a diary
in which he means to write one
story, and writes another.

J. M. Barrie

War does not
determine who is right
~ only who is left.
Bertrand Russell

Love, Marriage and Sex

Marriage is distinctly and
repeatedly excluded from heaven.
Is this because it is thought likely
to mar the general felicity?

Samuel Butler

Happiness in marriage is
entirely a matter of chance.

Jane Austen, *Pride and Prejudice*, **1813**

I never married because there was
no need. I have three pets at home
which answer the same purpose
as a husband. I have a dog which
growls every morning, a parrot
which swears all afternoon, and a
cat that comes home late at night.

Marie Corelli, writer (1855–1924)

It is a woman's business to get married as soon as possible, and a man's to keep unmarried as long as possible.

George Bernard Shaw

Marriage may often be a stormy lake, but celibacy is almost always a muddy horse pond.

Thomas Love Peacock, writer (1785–1866)

The course of true love never did run smooth.

William Shakespeare, *A Midsummer Night's Dream*

When my love swears that
she is made of truth,
I do believe her though
I know she lies.

William Shakespeare, Sonnet 138

———•———

Absence – that common
cure of love.

Lord Byron

———•———

A mistress never is nor can
be a friend. While you agree,
you are lovers; and when it is
over, anything but friends.

Lord Byron

Bachelors have consciences,
married men have wives.

Samuel Johnson

———•———

Ideally, couples need three
lives; one for him, one for her,
and one for them together.

Jacqueline Bisset, actress

———•———

When a man says he had
pleasure with a woman he does
not mean conversation.

Samuel Johnson

No woman ever hates a man
for being in love with her, but
many a woman hates a man
for being a friend to her.

Alexander Pope

———•———

And when a woman's will is as
strong as the man's who wants
to govern her, half her strength
must be concealment.

George Eliot, writer (1819–1880)

———•———

Love the quest; marriage the
conquest; divorce the inquest.

Helen Rowland

The most happy
marriage I can imagine
to myself would be
the union of a deaf
man to a blind woman.

Samuel Taylor Coleridge, poet, critic
and philosopher (1772–1834)

A man marries to have a home,
but also because he doesn't
want to be bothered with sex
and all that sort of thing.

W. Somerset Maugham

Marriage is a very good thing,
but I think it's a mistake to
make a habit out of it.

W. Somerset Maugham

Marriage is popular because
it combines the maximum
of temptation with the
maximum of opportunity.

George Bernard Shaw

Love is a wonderful, terrible thing.

William Shakespeare

Love comes unseen;
we only see it go.

**Austin Dobson, poet, critic and
biographer (1840–1921)**

My first words, as I was being
born... I looked up at my mother
and said, 'That's the last time
I'm going up one of those.'

Stephen Fry, actor and writer, on being gay

It is impossible to obtain a
conviction for sodomy from an
English jury. Half of them don't
believe that it can physically be
done, and the other half are doing it.

Winston Churchill

———•———

There is hardly anyone whose
sexual life, if it were broadcast,
would not fill the world at large
with surprise and horror.

W. Somerset Maugham

You know, of course, that the Tasmanians, who never committed adultery, are now extinct.

W. Somerset Maugham

———◆———

I've only slept with men I've been married to. How many women can make that claim?

Elizabeth Taylor

———◆———

Make love to every woman you meet; if you get five per cent of your outlay it's a good investment.

Arnold Bennett, novelist, playwright, critic and essayist (1867–1931)

I think being a woman
is like being Irish.
Everyone says
you're important
and nice, but you
take second place
all the same.

Iris Murdoch

The war between the sexes is
the only one in which both sides
regularly sleep with the enemy.
Quentin Crisp

———◆———

Pornography is the attempt to
insult sex, to do dirt on it.
D. H. Lawrence

———◆———

For flavour, instant sex will
never supersede the stuff
you have to peel and cook.
Quentin Crisp

If someone had told me years ago
that sharing a sense of humour
was so vital to partnerships, I
could have avoided a lot of sex.

Kate Beckinsale, actress

I'm a sex machine to both
genders. It's all very exhausting.
I need a lot of sleep.

Rupert Everett, actor

When sorrows
come, they come
not single spies,
But in battalions.

William Shakespeare, *Hamlet*

Media

Journalism is literature in a hurry.
Matthew Arnold, poet and critic (1822–1888)

———•———

In the old days men had the
rack, now they have the Press.
Oscar Wilde, *The Soul of Man Under Socialism*

———•———

A newspaper consists of just the
same number of words, whether
there be any news in it or not.
Henry Fielding, writer (1707–1754)

For fear of the newspapers
politicians are dull, and at
last they are too dull even
for the newspapers.

G. K. Chesterton

I review novels to make money,
because it is easier for a sluggard
to write an article a fortnight than
a book a year, because the writer
is soothed by the opiate of action,
the crank by posing as a good
journalist, and having an air hole.

Cyril Connolly, critic and editor (1903–1974)

A petty reason perhaps why
novelists more and more try to
keep a distance from journalists
is that novelists are trying to
write the truth and journalists
are trying to write fiction.

Graham Greene

———•———

Journalists say a thing that
they know isn't true, in the hope
that if they keep on saying it
long enough it will be true.

Arnold Bennett

He who is created by television
can be destroyed by television.

**Theodore H. White, journalist, historian
and novelist (1915–1986)**

Television has brought back murder
into the home – where it belongs.

Alfred Hitchcock, film director (1899–1980)

The most important service rendered by the press and the magazines is that of educating people to approach printed matter with distrust.

Samuel Butler

Seeing a murder on television can help work off one's antagonisms. And if you haven't any antagonisms, the commercials will give you some.

Alfred Hitchcock

The difference between literature and journalism is that journalism is unreadable, and literature is not read.

Oscar Wilde, *The Critic as Artist*, 1890

You are drunk Sir Winston, you are disgustingly drunk.

Yes, Mrs Braddock, I am drunk. But you, Mrs Braddock, are ugly, and disgustingly fat. But tomorrow morning, I, Winston Churchill will be sober.

Winston Churchill and Bessie Braddock, Labour MP (1899–1970)

Men and Women

Nature has given women so much power that the law has very wisely given them little.

Samuel Johnson

If all men are born free, how is it that all women are born slaves?

Mary Astell, feminist writer (1666–1731)

They say men can never experience the pain of childbirth. They can if you hit them in the goolies for fourteen hours.

Jo Brand

Some of my best leading men
have been dogs and horses.

Elizabeth Taylor

Men know that women are an
over-match for them, and therefore
they choose the weakest or most
ignorant. If they did not think so,
they never could be afraid of women
knowing as much as themselves.

Samuel Johnson

Men are judged as the sum
of their parts while women are
judged as some of their parts.

Julie Burchill

Women have a wonderful instinct
about things. They can discover
everything except the obvious.

Oscar Wilde, *An Ideal Husband*

———•———

It is difficult for a woman
to define her feelings in a
language which is chiefly made
by men to express theirs.

Thomas Hardy, novelist and poet (1840–1928)

———•———

God made woman beautiful
and foolish; beautiful, that man
might love her; and foolish,
that she might love him.

Anonymous

Most of us women like men, you know; it's just that we find them a constant disappointment.

Clare Short, politician

I would rather trust a woman's instinct than a man's reason.

Stanley Baldwin, politician and former Prime Minister (1867–1947)

I don't see why a man should think he is pleasing a woman enormously when he says to her a whole heap of things that he doesn't mean.

Oscar Wilde, *Lady Windermere's Fan*

Between men and
women there is no
friendship possible.
There is passion,
enmity, worship, love,
but no friendship.

Oscar Wilde, *Lady Windermere's Fan*

A wise woman puts
a grain of sugar
into everything she
says to a man, and
takes a grain of
salt with everything
he says to her.

Helen Rowland

Woman's dearest delight is
to wound Man's self-conceit,
though Man's dearest
delight is to gratify hers

George Bernard Shaw

And verily, a woman need know
but one man well, in order to
understand all men; whereas a
man may know all women and
understand not one of them.

Helen Rowland

Every man wants a woman to
appeal to his better side, his
nobler instincts and his higher
nature – and another woman
to help him forget them.

Helen Rowland

It is a truth universally acknowledged, that a single man in possession of a good fortune must be in want of a wife.

Jane Austen, *Pride and Prejudice*

Being a woman is a terribly difficult task, since it consists principally in dealing with men.

Joseph Conrad

I'm not denying the women are foolish: God Almighty made 'em to match the men.

George Eliot, *Adam Bede,* 1859

I equally dislike the favour of the public with the love of a woman – they are both a cloying treacle to the wings of independence.

John Keats, poet (1795–1821)

A misanthrope I can understand – a womanthrope never.

Oscar Wilde, *The Importance of Being Earnest*

'Tis strange what a man may do and a woman yet think him an angel.

William Makepeace Thackeray, Indian-born author and novelist (1811–1863)

Women are meant
to be loved, not to
be understood.

Oscar Wilde, *The Sphinx Without a Secret*

You can tell the strength of a
nation by the women behind its men.

Benjamin Disraeli

I was brought up among the sort
of self-important women who had
a husband as one has an alibi.

Anita Brookner, art historian and author

We women talk too much,
nevertheless we only say
half of what we know.

**Nancy Witcher Astor, politician and first woman to
sit in the British House of Commons (1879–1964)**

Clever and attractive women
do not want to vote; they are
willing to let men govern as
long as they govern men.

George Bernard Shaw

A woman, especially if she has the
misfortune of knowing anything,
should conceal it as well as she can.

Jane Austen, *Pride and Prejudice*

A woman, a dog and a walnut
tree, the more you beat
them, the better they be.

Thomas Fuller, writer and clergyman (1608–1661)

One of the things being in politics
has taught me is that men are not
a reasoned or reasonable sex.

Margaret Thatcher, politician and
former Prime Minister

Why are women so much
more interesting to men
than men are to women?

Virginia Woolf

———•—•———

The main difference between
men and women is that men are
lunatics and women are idiots.

Rebecca West, writer (1892–1983)

———•—•———

If there is anything
disagreeable going on, men
are sure to get out of it.

Jane Austen, *Northanger Abbey*

A complete woman is probably not a very admirable creature. She is manipulative, uses other people to get her own way, and works within whatever system she is in.

Anita Brookner

———✦———

I like women. I don't understand them, but I like them.

Sean Connery, actor, producer and film director

A prisoner of war
is a man who tries
to kill you and fails,
and then asks you
not to kill him.

Winston Churchill

Morals, Manners and Character

Integrity is so perishable in the summer months of success.

Vanessa Redgrave, actress

———•———

A long habit of not thinking a thing wrong gives it a superficial appearance of being right.

Thomas Paine

———•———

Character is much easier kept than recovered.

Thomas Paine

No man was ever great by imitation.
Samuel Johnson

———•———

No man can be a patriot
on an empty stomach.
William Cowper, poet (1731–1800)

———•———

Talk to every woman as if you
loved her, and to every man as if
he bored you, and at the end of
your first season you will have
the reputation of possessing
the most perfect social tact.
Oscar Wilde, *A Woman of No Importance*

I have often wished I had time to cultivate modesty. But I am too busy thinking about myself.

Edith Sitwell

———•———

Whatever it is that makes a person charming, it needs to remain a mystery. Once the charmer is aware of a mannerism or characteristic that others find charming, it ceases to be a mannerism and becomes an affectation. And good Lord, there is nothing less charming than affectations!

Rex Harrison, actor (1908–1990)

———•———

The test of real character is what a man does when he is tired.

Winston Churchill

With men he can be rational and unaffected, but when he has ladies to please, every feature works.

Jane Austen, *Emma*, 1815

———•———

The best measure of a man's honesty isn't his income tax return. It's the zero adjust on his bathroom scale.

Arthur C. Clarke, writer, broadcaster and explorer

———•———

I do not want people to be very agreeable, as it saves me the trouble of liking them a great deal.

Jane Austen

I am one of those unhappy
persons who inspire bores to
the greatest flights of art.

Edith Sitwell

———•———

Eating words has never
given me indigestion.

Winston Churchill

———•———

I am extraordinarily
patient, provided I get my
own way in the end.

Margaret Thatcher

A harmless hilarity and a buoyant
cheerfulness are not infrequent
concomitants of genius; and we
are never more deceived than
when we mistake gravity for
greatness, solemnity for science,
and pomposity for erudition.

Charles Caleb Colton

———

The man who lets himself
be bored is even more
contemptible than the bore.

Samuel Butler

Nine-tenths of the people were created so you would want to be with the other tenth.

Horace Walpole, writer (1717–1797)

Politics

To cure the British disease
with Socialism was like trying to
cure leukaemia with leeches.

Margaret Thatcher

———•———

No man is regular in his
attendance at the House of
Commons until he is married.

Benjamin Disraeli

———•———

History will be kind to me
for I intend to write it.

Winston Churchill

Oh don't you know, I'm the new tea lady round here.

Mo Mowlam, talking to Bill Clinton after being cold-shouldered by Tony Blair

---

The wisdom of hindsight, so useful to historians and indeed to authors of memoirs, is sadly denied to practising politicians.

Margaret Thatcher

Politics are very much like war. We may even have to use poison gas at times.

Winston Churchill

A Parliament is nothing
less than a big meeting of
more or less idle people.

Walter Bagehot

You can't be in politics unless
you can walk in a room and
know in a minute who's for
you and who's against you.

Samuel Johnson

I'm just preparing my
impromptu remarks.

Winston Churchill

In politics, there is no use looking
beyond the next fortnight.

Neville Chamberlain, politician and
former Prime Minister (1869–1940)

The Labour Party's election
manifesto is the longest
suicide note in history.

Greg Knight, Conservative MP

What do you want to
be a sailor for? There
are greater storms
in politics than you
will ever find at sea.
Piracy, broadsides,
blood on the decks.
You will find them
all in politics.

David Lloyd George

I have no interest in sailing around
the world. Not that there is any
lack of requests for me to do so.

**Edward Heath, politician and former
Prime Minister (1916–2005)**

If the word 'No' was removed
from the English language, Ian
Paisley would be speechless.

John Hume, politician

I adore political parties. They
are the only place left to us where
people don't talk politics.

Oscar Wilde, *An Ideal Husband*

I've given up voting: it seems
that whoever you vote for
the politicians always win.

Stewart Ferris, author, *Tish and Pish*

———•———

A politician is a person with whose
politics you don't agree; if you
agree with him he's a statesman.

David Lloyd George

———•———

What is politics but persuading
the public to vote for this and
support that and endure these
for the promise of those?

Gilbert Highet, classicist (1906–1978)

It seems to me
a barren thing
this conservatism
~ an unhappy cross
breed, the mule
of politics that
engenders nothing.

Benjamin Disraeli

A week is a long time in politics.

Harold Wilson, politican and former
Prime Minister (1916–1995)

———•———

There is no gambling like politics.

Benjamin Disraeli

I have never found in
a long experience of
politics that criticism
is ever inhibited
by ignorance.

Harold Macmillan, politician and former
Prime Minister (1894–1986)

You will find in politics that
you are much exposed to the
attribution of false motive. Never
complain and never explain.

Stanley Baldwin

———•———

He knows nothing and thinks he
knows everything. That clearly
points to a career in politics.

George Bernard Shaw

———•———

King Louis Philippe once said
to me that he attributed the
great success of the British
nation in political life to their
talking politics after dinner.

Benjamin Disraeli

All politics are based on the
indifference of the majority.

James Reston, journalist (1909–1995)

Politics we bar,
They are not our bent:
On the whole we are
Not intelligent.

William S. Gilbert, lyricist (1836–1911), *Princess Ida*, 1884

Our great democracies still
tend to think that a stupid man
is more likely to be honest than
a clever man, and our politicians
take advantage of this prejudice
by pretending to be even more
stupid than nature made them.

Bertrand Russell

A lot has been said about
politicians; some of it complimentary,
but most of it accurate.

Eric Idle, comedian, actor and film director

If politicians and scientists
were lazier, how much
happier we should all be.

Evelyn Waugh, writer (1903–1966)

The best time to listen to a politician is when he's on a stump on a street corner in the rain late at night when he's exhausted. Then he doesn't lie.

Theodore H. White

———◆———

I remain just one thing, and one thing only, and that is a clown. It places me on a far higher plane than any politician.

Charlie Chaplin

———◆———

A politician [...] one that would circumvent God.

William Shakespeare, *Hamlet*

Coffee which makes the politician
wise, and see through all things
with his half-shut eyes.

Alexander Pope

Where law ends, tyranny begins.

John Locke, philosopher (1632–1704)

Many politicians lay it down as a
self-evident proposition, that no
people ought to be free till they are
fit to use their freedom. The maxim
is worthy of the fool in the old story,
who resolved not to go into the
water till he had learned to swim.

Thomas Babington Macaulay, historian (1800–1859)

The proper memory for a politician is one that knows what to remember and what to forget.

John Morley, journalist, biographer
and statesman (1838–1923)

If people want a sense of purpose they should get it from their archbishop. They should certainly not get it from their politicians.

Harold Macmillan

The difference between a
misfortune and a calamity is
this: If Gladstone fell into the
Thames, it would be a misfortune.
But if someone dragged him out
again, that would be a calamity.

Benjamin Disraeli

Politics is a blood sport.

Aneurin Bevan

Imagination was given
to man to compensate
him for what he
is not; a sense of
humour to console
him for what he is.

Francis Bacon

Religion

A good sermon should be like
a woman's skirt: short enough
to arouse interest but long
enough to cover the essentials.

Ronald Knox, writer and theologian (1888–1957)

When did I realise I was God?
Well, I was praying and I suddenly
realised I was talking to myself.

Peter O'Toole, Irish born actor and director

Religion is the fashionable
substitute for belief.

Oscar Wilde, *The Picture of Dorian Gray*

When the Gods want to punish
us, they answer our prayers.
Oscar Wilde

———

So far as I can remember, there
is not one word in the Gospels
in praise of intelligence.
Bertrand Russell

———

The devil can cite
Scripture for his purpose.
William Shakespeare, *The Merchant of Venice*

He wears his faith but as
the fashion of his hat.

William Shakespeare, *Much Ado About Nothing*

If there were no God, there
would be no Atheists.

G. K. Chesterton

The Christian ideal has not been
tried and found wanting; it has been
found difficult and left untried.

G. K. Chesterton

God is a concept by which
we measure our pain.

John Lennon

———•———

The belief in a supernatural source
of evil is not necessary; men alone are
quite capable of every wickedness.

Joseph Conrad

———•———

The religion of one seems
madness unto another.

Thomas Browne, physician and writer (1605–1682)

No mention of God. They
keep Him up their sleeves for
as long as they can, vicars do.
They know it puts people off.

Alan Bennett

———•———

Fear of things invisible is the
natural seed of that which everyone
in himself calleth religion.

Thomas Hobbes, philosopher (1588–1679)

Isn't it enough to
see that a garden
is beautiful without
having to believe that
there are fairies at
the bottom of it too?

Douglas Adams

The more I study religions the
more I am convinced that man never
worshipped anything but himself.

Richard Francis Burton, explorer (1821–1890)

———•———

No man ever believes that
the Bible means what it says:
He is always convinced that
it says what he means.

George Bernard Shaw

———•———

Why should we take advice on
sex from the Pope? If he knows
anything about it, he shouldn't!

George Bernard Shaw

Heaven, as conventionally
conceived, is a place so inane,
so dull, so useless, so miserable
that nobody has ever ventured to
describe a whole day in heaven,
though plenty of people have
described a day at the seaside.

George Bernard Shaw

———————

The worst of madmen
is a saint run mad.

Alexander Pope

———————

Religion is an attempt to get an
irrefragably safe investment, and
this cannot be got, no matter how
low the interest, which in the case of
religion is about as low as it can be.

Samuel Butler

Sailors ought never to go to church. They ought to go to hell, where it is much more comfortable.

H. G. Wells

He hoped and prayed that there wasn't an afterlife. Then he realised there was a contradiction involved here and merely hoped that there wasn't an afterlife.

Douglas Adams

I simply haven't the nerve to imagine a being, a force, a cause which keeps the planets revolving in their orbits and then suddenly stops in order to give me a bicycle with three speeds.

Quentin Crisp

———◆———

Faith goes out through the window when beauty comes in at the door.

George Moore

Like all great
travellers, I have seen
more than I remember,
and remember more
than I have seen.

Benjamin Disraeli

Science

New ideas pass through three periods: 1) It can't be done. 2) It probably can be done, but it's not worth doing. 3) I knew it was a good idea all along!

Arthur C. Clarke

———•———

I don't believe in astrology; I'm a Sagittarius and we're sceptical.

Arthur C. Clarke

———•———

Civilisation advances by extending the number of important operations which we can perform without thinking.

Alfred North Whitehead, mathematician and philosopher (1861–1947)

It is a safe rule to apply that, when
a mathematical or philosophical
author writes with a misty
profundity, he is talking nonsense.

Alfred North Whitehead

If all feeling for grace and beauty
were not extinguished in the mass of
mankind at the actual moment, such
a method of locomotion as cycling
could never have found acceptance;
no man or woman with the slightest
aesthetic sense could assume the
ludicrous position necessary for it.

Ouida

A computer terminal is not
some clunky old television with
a typewriter in front of it. It is an
interface where the mind and body
can connect with the universe
and move bits of it about.

Douglas Adams

The great tragedy of science:
the slaying of a beautiful
hypothesis by an ugly fact.

Thomas Henry Huxley, biologist (1825–1895)

Before a war military science
seems like a real science, like
astronomy; but after a war it
seems more like astrology.

Rebecca West

Science is the great antidote
to the poison of enthusiasm
and superstition.

Adam Smith

Ignorance more frequently begets confidence than does knowledge: it is those who know little, and not those who know much, who so positively assert that this or that problem will never be solved by science.

Charles Darwin, naturalist (1809–1882)

Logic is neither a science or an art, but a dodge.

Benjamin Jowett, Classical scholar (1817–1893)

Science has its being in a perpetual mental restlessness.

William Temple, theologian (1628–1699)

If it looks like a duck,
and quacks like a
duck, we have at
least to consider
the possibility that
we have a small
aquatic bird of the
family anatidae
on our hands.

Douglas Adams

Vices

The greatest art of a politician
is to render vice serviceable
to the cause of virtue.

Henry Bolingbroke, politician (1678–1751)

Vice, in its true light, is so
deformed, that it shocks us at
first sight; and would hardly ever
seduce us, if it did not at first
wear the mask of some virtue.

Lord Chesterfield

Murder is always a mistake. One
should never do anything that one
cannot talk about after dinner.

Oscar Wilde, *The Picture of Dorian Gray*

As one reads history... one is
absolutely sickened, not by
the crimes that the wicked have
committed, but by the punishments
that the good have inflicted:
A community is infinitely more
brutalised by the habitual
employment of punishment
than it is by the occasional
occurrence of crime.

Oscar Wilde, *The Soul of Man Under Socialism*

That the world is overrun with
vice cannot be denied; but vice,
however predominant, has not yet
gained an unlimited dominion.

Samuel Johnson: *Rambler* #119, 7 May, 1751

The problem with people who have
no vices is that generally you can
be pretty sure they're going to
have some pretty annoying virtues.

Elizabeth Taylor

———

Let them show me a cottage where
there are not the same vices of
which they accuse the courts.

Lord Chesterfield

———

The faults of the burglar are
the qualities of the financier.

George Bernard Shaw

Every day confirms my opinion
on the superiority of a vicious
life – and if Virtue is not its
own reward I don't know any
other stipend annexed to it.

Lord Byron

He who is only just is cruel.
Who on earth could live
were all judged justly?

Lord Byron

Flippancy, the most hopeless
form of intellectual vice.

George Gissing, novelist (1857–1903)

The function of vice is to keep
virtue within reasonable bounds.

Samuel Butler

I sometimes think
that God, in creating
man, somewhat
overestimated
his ability.

Attributed to Oscar Wilde

Virtues

Plain dealing is a jewel, but they
that wear it are out of fashion.

Thomas Fuller

———•———

Virtue is a beautiful thing in
woman when they don't go about
with it like a child with a drum
making all sorts of noise with it.

**Douglas Jerrold, humorist, playwright
and journalist (1803–1857)**

———•———

Assume a virtue if you have not it.

William Shakespeare, *Hamlet*

I always admired virtue – but
I could never imitate it.

King Charles II (1630–1685)

Patience, that blending of moral
courage with physical timidity.

Thomas Hardy

Liberty means responsibility.
That is why most men dread it.

George Bernard Shaw

Virtue is more to be feared
than vice, because its excesses
are not subject to the
regulation of conscience.

Adam Smith

———•———

Virtue is too often merely local.

Samuel Johnson

———•———

Virtue is its own punishment.

Aneurin Bevan

Nobody shoots at Santa Claus.

Samuel Butler

———•———

Plenty of people wish to
become devout, but no one
wishes to be humble.

Joseph Addison, writer (1672–1719)

———•———

Vices and virtues are of a strange
nature, for the more we have,
the fewer we think we have.

Alexander Pope

In England the only homage which
they pay to Virtue – is hypocrisy.

Lord Byron

———•———

Moderation has been called a virtue
to limit the ambition of great men,
and to console undistinguished
people for their want of fortune
and their lack of merit.

Benjamin Disraeli

Blessed is the man who, having nothing to say, abstains from giving us wordy evidence of the fact.

George Eliot

If he does really think that there is no distinction between virtue and vice, why, Sir, when he leaves our houses let us count our spoons.

Samuel Johnson

I'd stay away from Ecstasy. This is a drug so powerful it makes white people think they can dance.

Lenny Henry, comedian

Work, Money and Success

A celebrity is one who is known to many persons he is glad he doesn't know.

Lord Byron

———•———

Actors never retire, they just get less and less work.

Desmond Llewelyn, actor (1914–1999)

———•———

A fan club is a group of people who tell an actor he's not alone in the way he feels about himself.

Kenneth Williams, actor and comic (1926–1988)

My parents felt that acting was
far too insecure. Don't ask
me what made them think that
painting would be more secure.

John Hurt, actor

———•———

I paint for myself. I don't know
how to do anything else,
anyway. Also I have to earn
my living, and occupy myself.

Francis Bacon, artist (1919–1992)

———•———

Experience shows that success
is due less to ability than to zeal.

Charles Buxton, writer (1823–1871)

In many walks of life, a conscience
is a more expensive encumbrance
than a wife or a carriage.

Thomas De Quincey, writer (1785–1859)

———•———

A thing is worth what it can
do for you, not what you
choose to pay for it.

John Ruskin

———•———

If at first you don't succeed,
failure may be your style.

Quentin Crisp

Love lasteth long as the
money endureth.

William Caxton, printer, translator
and publisher (1422–1491)

———•———

Money is like a sixth sense
– and you can't make use of
the other five without it.

W. Somerset Maugham

An agent is a person who is sore because an actor gets 90 per cent of what they make.

Elton John, singer and songwriter

———◆———

A large income is the best recipe for happiness I ever heard of.

Jane Austen, *Mansfield Park*, 1814

Neither irony or
sarcasm is argument.

Samuel Butler

Youth

The excesses of our youth
are checks written against
our age and they are payable
with interest 30 years later.

Charles Caleb Colton

Human nature is so well disposed
towards those who are in interesting
situations, that a young person,
who either marries or dies, is
sure of being kindly spoken of.

Jane Austen, *Emma*

The young always have the same
problem – how to rebel and conform
at the same time. They have
now solved this by defying their
parents and copying one another.

Quentin Crisp

What Youth deemed crystal,
Age finds out was dew.

Robert Browning, poet (1812–1889)

Youth is the time of getting,
middle age of improving, and
old age of spending.

Anne Bradstreet, poet (1612–1672)

The young have aspirations
that never come to pass, the
old have reminiscences of
what never happened.

Saki

A man loves the meat in his youth
that he cannot endure in his age.
William Shakespeare, *Much Ado About Nothing*

———•———

Young men and young women meet
each other with much less difficulty
than was formerly the case, and
every housemaid expects at least
once a week as much excitement as
would have lasted a Jane Austen
heroine throughout a whole novel.
Bertrand Russell

Mr Churchill, if you
were my husband,
I'd poison your tea!

And if you were my
wife, I'd drink it!

Winston Churchill and Nancy Astor, Tory MP (1879–1964)

---

www.summersdale.com